Forty sparkling quizzes on the most trivial aspects of quotations. Designed to delight, bemuse and bewilder, QUOTABLE TRIVIA is a quiz-book in which the answers are infinitely more interesting than the questions! What's more, the daftest answers are usually the right ones!

Also available:

SHOWBIZ TRIVIA
SIXTIES TRIVIA

NIGEL REES

London
UNWIN PAPERBACKS
Boston Sydney

First published by Unwin Paperbacks, 1985

UNWIN® PAPERBACKS
40 Museum Street, London WC1A 1LU, UK

Unwin Paperbacks
Park Lane, Hemel Hempstead, Herts HP2 4TE, UK

George Allen & Unwin Australia Pty Ltd
8 Napier Street, North Sydney, NSW 2060, Australia

Unwin Paperbacks with the
Port Nicholson Press
PO Box 11-838 Wellington, New Zealand

ISBN 0 04 793083 7

Set in 10 on 11 point Souvenir by Nene Phototypesetters Ltd
and printed in Great Britain by
The Anchor Press Ltd, Tiptree, Essex

For Vernon Noble

CONTENTS

PREFACE

When I started my radio quiz *Quote . . . Unquote* ten years ago, I rapidly discovered that there were only about twelve quotations that any fairly intelligent person might be expected to know. *This book does not contain them.*

It is made up of the bric-à-brac . . . the somewhat erudite and *outré* quotations used, for the most part, in the ninth and tenth series of the radio show.

You probably won't know the answers, but have a try. Do a bit of detective work. Ask yourself 'What century does this quotation *seem* to be from?' 'Does it sound like a man or a woman speaking?' 'What sort of job are they likely to have had?'

Very often you will discover that the most obvious answer is the right one.

NIGEL REES

QUESTIONS

1

AUTHOR! AUTHOR!

1 'Another damned, thick, square book! Always scribble, scribble, scribble! Eh! Mr ———' A Duke of Gloucester said this to a famous historian on being given a second volume. Who was the author?

2 Which writer made a curtain speech at Drury Lane in which he said: 'In spite of the troublous times we are living in, it is still pretty exciting to be English'?

3 Which poet said: 'A good book is the precious life-blood of a master spirit, embalmed and treasured up on purpose to a life beyond life'?

4 Who posthumously addressed his public with the words, 'Now I stretch out my hand, and from the further shore I bid adieu to all who have cared to read any among the words that I have written', and rather shocked it at the same time?

5 Which poet talked of 'A tale which holdeth children from play and old men from the chimney corner'?

6 Who said: 'A man will turn over half a library to make one book'?

7 Who said: 'When I want to read a novel I write one'?

8 Who described his function thus: 'I am a camera with its shutter open, quite passive, recording, not thinking'?

9 Who began his book: 'The first thing you'll probably want to know is where I was born, and what my childhood was like, and how my parents were occupied . . . and all that David Copperfield kind of crap'?

10 Which fictional author was asked – in a film – 'Do you just do your writing now – or are you still working'?

2

BOOK TITLES

Where were these titles taken from?

1 *The Sea, The Sea,* Iris Murdoch.

2 *One Brief Shining Moment,* William Manchester.

3 *None But the Lonely Heart,* Richard Llewellyn.

4 *The Moon and Sixpence,* Somerset Maugham.

5 *The End of the World News,* Anthony Burgess.

6 *The Heart is a Lonely Hunter,* Carson McCullers.

7 *God Stand Up for Bastards,* David Leitch.

8 *The Strangers All Are Gone,* Anthony Powell.

9 *Ancestral Vices,* Tom Sharpe.

10 *Dear Lord Rothschild,* Miriam Rothschild.

3

CATCHPHRASES

Whose catchphrase is or was:

1 'Not many people know that.'

2 'You cannot be serious.'

3 'It's all done in the best possible taste.'

4 'Move 'em on, head 'em up.'

5 'Exterminate . . . exterminate!'

6 'The ——fulness is terrific.'

7 'Gi' us a job.'

8 'I am not a number. I am a free man.'

9 'Oh, my Sunday helmet!'

10 'Drop the gun, Looey!'

4

CELEBRITIES

. . . on themselves . . .

1 What poet said of himself: 'My face looks like a wedding-cake left out in the rain'?

2 What actor said of himself: 'I have a face like the behind of an elephant'?

3 What writer said of one of his lesser-known attributes: 'It's all very well to be able to write books, but can you wiggle your ears'?

4 What famous son said of himself: 'I should never be allowed out in private'?

5 What film star said of himself: 'I have a face that is a cross between two pounds of halibut and an explosion in an old-clothes closet. If it isn't mobile, it's dead'?

6 What writer said of himself: 'I have always been a grumbler. I am designed for the part – sagging face, weighty underlip, rumbling, resonant voice. Money couldn't buy a better grumbling outfit'?

7 What broadcaster suggested this epitaph for himself: 'He never used a sentence where a paragraph would do'?

8 What singer said of himself: 'I always feel my voice is like black velvet on sandpaper'?

9 What politician said of himself: 'If the fence is strong enough, I'll sit on it'?

10 What woman said of herself: 'I am the Mary Poppins of Israel'?

CHURCHILLIANA

1 About whom did Churchill say, '[He is] like a female llama surprised in her bath'?

2 Sir Alfred Munnings RA claimed that Churchill once said to him, 'Alfred, if you met ——— coming down the street, would you join with me in kicking his something something?' Met who?

3 Harold Nicolson noted in his diary for 20 August 1940 that Churchill said, 'Never in the history of human conflict has so much been owed by so many to so few' – did he really?

4 About whose memorandum did he deny saying, 'As far as I can see, you have used every cliché except "God is love" and "Please adjust your dress before leaving"'?

5 Why did he say 'Dead birds don't fall out of nests'?

6 Whom did he deny describing as 'a sheep in sheep's clothing'?

7 Which other Prime Minister did he call 'The Boneless Wonder'?

8 With what words did he begin his first public speech?

9 What did he describe as 'a remarkable example of modern art'?

10 Who said of Churchill that he 'mobilised the English language and sent it into battle'?

6

COMPLETE THE QUOTE

1 'The life of man, solitary, poor . . .' (Thomas Hobbes, *Leviathan*).

2 'No matter how thin you slice it, it's still . . .' (Alfred E. Smith).

3 'What's good for General Motors is . . .' (Charles E. Wilson).

4 'Acting is easy, as long as you learn your lines and . . .' (Noel Coward).

5 'All animals are equal, but . . .' (George Orwell).

6 'But soon a wonder came to light
That showed the rogues they lied;
The man recover'd of the bite . . .'
(Oliver Goldsmith).

7 'In any hierarchy, an employee rises to his . . .' (Laurence J. Peter).

8 'A Book of Verses underneath the Bough
A Jug of Wine, a Loaf of Bread and . . .'
(Edward Fitzgerald).

9 'France has lost a battle, but . . .' (Charles de Gaulle).

10 'Please accept my resignation. I don't wish to belong to any club that . . .' (Groucho Marx).

7

CRITICAL OPINIONS

1 What first night led Anthony Hope to exclaim: 'Oh, for an hour of Herod!'?

2 Of what did Sir Thomas Beecham say: 'What can you do with it? It's like a lot of yaks jumping about'?

3 What symphony did Sir Thomas Beecham describe as 'the musical equivalent of St Pancras station'?

4 Who was Artur Lundkvist describing when he called his works 'A little English phenomenon of no special interest'?

5 In 1908, about what novel did the *Times Literary Supplement* opine: 'As a contribution to natural history the work is negligible'?

6 Of what British performer did an American critic state in 1979 – 'He'll be a riot at your friend's wedding, but not on Broadway'?

7 Of which composer's music did Oscar Wilde say, 'It is so loud, one can talk the whole time without other people hearing what one says'?

8 Which author's work did D. H. Lawrence describe as 'Nothing but old fags and cabbage-stumps of quotations from the Bible and the rest, served in the juice of deliberate journalistic dirty-mindedness'?

9 What book by Edward Heath did critic Christopher Wordsworth slate as: 'A reminder that Morning Cloud's skipper is no stranger to platitude and longitude'?

10 Of Beerbohm Tree's performance in which play did W. S. Gilbert say that it was: 'Funny, without being vulgar'?

CROSSWORDS

. . . and a puzzle . . .

1 ‘ABCDEFGPQRSTUVWXYZ’ (9)

2 ‘1,000 in 1,200’ (10)

3 ‘Mechanical device for the alleviation of childbearing’ (4)

4 ‘Foreign entanglements’ (9)

5 ‘Limit of human understanding’ (3–4)

6 ‘The end of a line of angry monarchs’ (5,5)

7 ‘——————’ (*Love’s Labour’s Lost*) (27)

8 ‘GTIDS’ (7)

9 ‘Kill mother for the estate’ (6)

10 ‘What animal has four feet, then two feet, then three feet and only one voice? Its feet vary and when it has most it is weakest.’ The answer is ‘man’. So what is this?

EPITAPHS

1 'Though I sang in my chains like the sea' – he wrote it, and it's on his memorial in Westminster Abbey. Who is he?

2 On whose grave in Rome does it say, 'Here lies one whose name was writ with water', but does not reveal his name?

3 'I'm saying, here I am now. How are you? How's your relationship going? Did you get through it all? Wasn't the Seventies a drag? Here we are, let's try to make it through the Eighties, you know' – who said that a few days before he died?

4 'I can't think of a more wonderful thanksgiving for the life I have had, than that everyone should be jolly at my funeral' – but it was not possible. Who said that in his own pre-recorded obituary?

5 Who was 'coughing well tonight' but has 'After life's fitful fever he sleeps well' on his grave in Warrington?

6 'I've been to the mountain top. I've looked over and seen the promised land' – who said that the day before he died?

7 On whose monument does it say 'Patriotism is not enough'?

8 Dr Johnson said of whose death that it had 'eclipsed the gaiety of nations and impoverished the public stock of harmless pleasure'?

9 On whose tomb in Dublin is it stated that he is now 'where fierce indignation can no longer tear his heart'?

10 What does the tomb inscription 'Et in Arcadia, ego' mean?

FAMOUS PHRASES

The origins, please, of these well-known phrases . . .

1 'Nature, red in tooth and claw'.

2 'Night of the long knives'.

3 'A desperate disease requires a dangerous remedy'.

4 'Life begins at forty'.

5 'Long hot summer'.

6 'It takes two to tango'.

7 'Fings ain't wot they used t'be'.

8 'Lady with the lamp'.

9 'The Dark Continent'.

10 'It's all part of life's rich pageant'.

FILM QUOTES

In which film:

1 Is this line *not* spoken – 'A long time ago, in a galaxy far, far away . . .'?

2 Is this line spoken by Terry-Thomas – 'You've made a happy man feel very old'?

3 Is this line spoken to Ben Lyon – 'Would you be shocked if I put on something more comfortable'?

4 Is this line spoken, although it does not occur in the original book – 'Frankly, my dear, I don't give a damn'?

5 Does an actress deliver these lines – her first spoken ones on the screen – 'Gimme a viskey – ginger ale on the side. And don't be stingy, baby'?

6 Does an actress ever so slightly change what a real-life character said – 'I know I have the body of a weak and feeble woman, but I have the heart and valour of a king'?

7 Does Elliott ask – 'How do you explain school to a higher intelligence'?

8 Does a king remark – 'The things I've done for England!'?

9 Does Marcel Marceau say 'Non!'?

10 Does a character say – according to Dirk Bogarde – 'Hiya, Chopin, this is my great friend Georges Sand. She's a great friend of Beethoven'?

12

FILM TITLES

Where did these films take their titles from – apart, that is, from any book or play they may have been based on?

1 *Heaven's Gate.*

2 *Another Country.*

3 *Ill Fares the Land.*

4 *Love Is a Many-Splendored Thing.*

5 *Whistle Down the Wind.*

6 *Something Wicked This Way Comes.*

7 *Angels One Five.*

8 *Chariots of Fire.*

9 *In Which We Serve.*

10 *Chimes at Midnight.*

FIRST WORDS

1 Of what are these the first words: 'It was a dark and stormy night'? (Clue: there are at least three possible answers.)

2 Whose autobiography begins, 'I was born in 1896, and my parents were married in 1919'?

3 After what significant event did J. Robert Oppenheimer quote: 'I am become death, the destroyer of worlds'?

4 Complete the following and say who wrote it: 'Not all that long ago, when children were even smaller and people had especially hairy knees, there lived an . . .'

5 Whose first words, in connection with what, were these: 'We have discovered the secret of life'?

6 'What can you say about a 25-year-old girl who died? That she was beautiful. And brilliant. That she loved Mozart and Bach. And the Beatles. And me' – are the opening words of which novel?

7 'Our long national nightmare is over' – what sort of nightmare?

8 'Mr Watson, come here, I want you!' were the first intelligible words transmitted over a telephone. Who said them?

9 'What hath God wrought' are sometimes said to be the words used in the first successful telegraph message. They weren't – but who sent them?

10 'We knocked the bastard off!' – who had? And what was it?

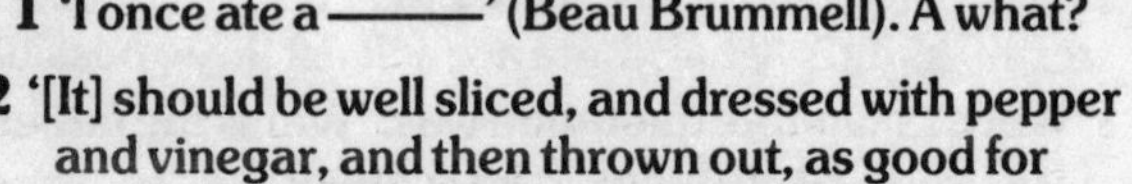

14

FOOD

1 'I once ate a ——' (Beau Brummell). A what?

2 '[It] should be well sliced, and dressed with pepper and vinegar, and then thrown out, as good for nothing' (Dr Johnson). What should?

3 In Shakespeare's *The Winter's Tale*, Autolycus says of his father that he was 'a snapper-up of unconsidered ——'?

4 'I raised to my lips a spoonful of the tea in which I had soaked a morsel . . . suddenly the memory [returned].' A morsel of what?

5 Someone said to Somerset Maugham that he hated the food in England. Maugham replied, 'What rubbish! All you have to do is eat —— three times a day.' Eat what?

6 'It is a good fruit. You eat, you drink, you wash your face' (Enrico Caruso). What was he talking about?

7 'The noblest of all dogs is the —— ——; it feeds the hand that bites it.' (Laurence J. Peter)

8 'When I ask for a —— ——, I do not mean a loaf with a field in the middle of it.' (Oscar Wilde)

9 'I'm afraid you've got a bad ——, Mr Jones.' (*Punch*, 1895)

10 'You can tell a lot about a fellow's character by the way he eats —— ——.' (Ronald Reagan)

15

JUST FANCY THAT

1 Whose favourite quotation was: 'War is the father of all things' (Heraclitus)?

2 Which British politician's favourite quotation is: 'The Lord will provide [a beast for sacrifice]'?

3 Whose favourite quotation is: 'Leads you to believe a lie/When you see with, not thro' the eye'?

4 After what quotation is 'The Doors' pop group named?

5 Give two possible sources for the title of Sir William Walton's march 'Crown Imperial'.

6 'One picture is worth a thousand words' is a Chinese proverb. True or false?

7 General MacArthur said, 'I shall return,' on Australian soil, not in the Philippines. True or false?

8 Who, in his diary, was unable to spell 'prerogative' (and he should have known because he had one)?

9 To which poem have Olivia Newton-John and Frankie Goes To Hollywood alluded?

10 What did Neil Armstrong *intend* to say as he stepped on to the moon?

16

LAST WORDS

1 Whose dying words were, 'It's all been rather lovely,' and announced he had 'conked out' in *The Times* personal column?

2 Who sang the exit line, ''Scuse me while I disappear,' and then came back?

3 What ended for a while with a Garbo impersonator saying, 'Ah tink ah go home'?

4 When Edmund Gwenn, the actor, was dying, he was asked if it was hard. 'Yes,' he replied, 'but not as difficult as ———' What?

5 Which actor on his deathbed was asked by his son if he had any regrets and replied: 'Yes. Just one. I never got the Kipling cakes commercial'?

6 Who said, 'Je vais à la gloire,' and loosened her scarf?

7 When her family gathered round her deathbed, she inquired, 'Am I dying, or is it my birthday?' Who was she?

8 'If I knew I was going to live to this age [100], I'd have taken better care of myself' – name two people who have made this remark.

9 'The world shall hear from me again!' – said a (fictional) character who had just been blown up – and it did. Who was he?

10 'One may be optimistic, but one can't exactly be joyful at the prospect before us' – in what way were these words the end of civilisation as he knew it?

MISQUOTES

1 Which of his poetic lines was misquoted on Robert Louis Stevenson's grave in Samoa?

2 Which of Laurence Binyon's poetic lines is misquoted on a war memorial in Staines, Middlesex?

3 Cilla Black recorded 'Rule Britannia'. She sang 'Rule, Britannia,/Britannia rules the waves;/Britons never, never, never/Shall be slaves'. Why shouldn't she have done?

4 'Abandon hope, all ye who enter here' was not written over the entrance to Hell in Dante's *Inferno*, was it?

5 You would never sing 'For the sake of auld lang syne', would you?

6 Harold Wilson was quoted in 1948 as saying, 'The school I went to in the north was a school where more than half the children in my class never had any boots or shoes to their feet' – what was wrong with that?

7 During the trial of Jeremy Thorpe in 1979 his counsel said to the jury: 'I end by saying in the words of the Bible – "Let this prosecution fold up its tent and quietly creep away".' What had he got wrong?

8 'We are the masters now' is not precisely what Sir Hartley Shawcross said of the Labour Government in 1946. What did he say?

9 'Water, water, everywhere and not a drop to drink' should read . . . ?

10 'Tomorrow to fresh fields and pastures new' should read . . . ?

18

MOTTOES

1 Where would you find the motto 'Decus et tutamen'?

2 What organisation has the motto 'In utmost good faith'?

3 Name three people or organisations who have used the motto 'Fay ce que voudras' – 'Do what you will'.

4 Whose (unofficial) motto is 'Publish and be sued'?

5 Whose motto is 'Adopt–Adapt–Improve'?

6 Whose motto is 'Maintiens le droit' although they also 'always get their man'?

7 'Who Dares Wins' – who does?

8 'Mercatores coenascent' ('May the traders be convivial together') is the motto of which supermarket chain? (Clue: there is a pun in the second Latin word.)

9 Over the entrance to which holiday camp, in 1936, would you have seen: 'Our true intent is all for your delight'?

10 Which organisation has the motto 'Fidelity, Bravery, Integrity'?

19

NEWS HEADLINES

What did these famous newspaper headlines refer to?

1 'EGGHEAD WEDS HOURGLASS' (*Variety*)

2 'DR FUCHS OFF TO SOUTH ICE'

3 'DEWEY DEFEATS TRUMAN' (*Chicago Tribune*)

4 'KING'S MOLL RENO'S IN WOLSEY'S HOME TOWN' (American newspaper)

5 'GOTCHA!' (*Sun*)

6 'STICKS PIX NIX HICKS' (*Variety*)

7 'QUEEN IN BRAWL AT PALACE' (*Guardian*)

8 'THE END OF THE WORLD' (*Scottish Daily Express*)

9 'WALL STREET LAYS AN EGG' (*Variety*)

10 'SMALL EARTHQUAKE IN CHILE. NOT MANY DEAD.' (*The Times*)

20

PLACES

1 'From ———, Hell and ———, Good Lord Deliver us.' (The thieves'/beggars'/vagabonds' litany, dating from the sixteenth century.)

2 'If only I could get down to ———. I've been waiting for the weather to break.' (*The Caretaker*, Harold Pinter)

3 'The glory that was ——— and the grandeur that was ———.' (Edgar Allan Poe)

4 'I look upon ——— as an inferior sort of Scotland.' (Revd Sydney Smith)

5 'I saw a notice which said "Drink ——— Dry" and I've just started.' (Brendan Behan)

6 'Worth seeing, but not worth going to see' (Samuel Johnson). What was?

7 'I was the toast of two continents: ——— and ———.' (Dorothy Parker)

8 'Sir, a man who is tired of ——— is tired of life.' (Samuel Johnson)

9 'The shortest way out of ——— is notoriously a bottle of Gordon's Gin.' (William Bolitho)

10 '*On the Beach* is a story about the end of the world and ——— is sure the right place to film it.' (Attributed to Ava Gardner)

POETRY

. . . and poets . . .

1 In what poem would you find the line, 'Hold off! unhand me, grey-beard loon'?

2 'Rose is a rose is a rose is a rose' – but what did he do?

3 Who wrote the line, 'Not waving but drowning'?

4 How did 'The life that I have is all that I have/And the life that I have is yours' help the war effort?

5 Which Poet Laureate wrote the lines: 'Across the wires the electric message came;/He is no better, he is much the same'?

6 Which Poet Laureate replied, when asked in the last year of his life if he had any regrets: 'Yes, I haven't had enough sex'?

7 Which poet wrote concerning another that there would be: 'Never glad confident morning again'?

8 How many daffodils did Wordsworth see?

9 How many maids with mops might sweep what for half a year?

10 How many rows of beans did Yeats say he would have at Innisfree?

22

POLITICS

1 Who said, 'When they circumcised Herbert Samuel they threw away the wrong bit'?

2 Where was Gough Whitlam standing when he said, 'Well may he say "God Save the Queen" because nothing will save the Governor-General'?

3 What political office was John Nance Garner describing when he said it 'Isn't worth a pitcher of warm piss'?

4 Which military figure said of the 17th Earl of Derby, a politician, that he 'Like the feather pillow, bears the marks of the last person who sat on him'?

5 Which politician changed his name twice and said that if the British public voted Labour in 1964 it would be 'Stark, staring bonkers'?

6 Which politician threatened 'We will bury you'?

7 Which politician assured a friend that 'Bunnies *can* and *will* go to France'?

8 Who said, 'The first essential for a Prime Minister is to be a good butcher'?

9 Who, briefly, presided over 'Communism with a human face'?

10 Whose father 'Did not riot. He got on his bike and looked for work. And he kept on looking till he found it'?

23

PRESIDENTS

Which US President:

1 Said: 'Hawae the lads!' in 1977?

2 Said: 'If you can't stand the smell, keep out of the shit-house' – though he is usually quoted as saying something milder?

3 Caused Queen Elizabeth the Queen Mother to say: 'He is the only man since my dear husband died to have the effrontery to kiss me on the lips'?

4 Explained how he came to be a hero with the words: 'It was easy – they sank my boat'?

5 Explained: 'Mr Nixon was the thirty-seventh President of the United States. He had been preceded by thirty-six others'?

6 Said: 'You fellows, in your business, you have a way of handling problems like this. Somebody leaves a pistol in the drawer. I don't have a pistol'?

7 Said: 'I shall not seek and I will not accept the nomination of my party for another term as your President'?

8 Who, on being re-elected, declared: 'You ain't seen nothin' yet'?

9 Often said: 'I've got his pecker in my pocket'?

10 Famously said: 'The only thing we have to fear is fear itself'?

PRIME MINISTERS

. . . of Britain . . .

1 Who said of David Lloyd George, 'Ah, si pouvais pisser comme il parle' ('If only I could piss the way he talks')?

2 Who said of Neville Chamberlain that he was 'a good mayor of Birmingham in an off-year'?

3 Of which Prime Minister was it said, 'He died – as he lived – at sea'?

4 About which Prime Minister did Winston Churchill say, 'Not dead. But the candle in that great turnip has gone out'?

5 About which Prime Minister did H. H. Asquith say, 'It is fitting that we should have buried the Unknown Prime Minister by the side of the Unknown Soldier'?

6 Which Prime Minister wrote of himself:

Few thought he was even a starter
There were many who thought himself smarter.
But he ended PM, CH, and OM,
An Earl and a Knight of the Garter.

7 Which PM said of himself, 'I see myself as a deep-lying half-back feeding the ball forward to the chaps who score the goals'?

8 To which PM did Nigel Birch MP say, 'It will never be glad confident morning again for you or your government'?

9 In 1938, Cyril Connolly wrote of which future PM: 'He appeared honourably ineligible for the struggle of life'?

10 Which Prime Minister opined: 'Nothing matters very much and most things don't matter at all'?

PROPHETIC REMARKS

1 Which politician said in 1940: 'Hitler has missed the bus'?

2 Which inventor said in 1926: 'I have determined that there is no market for talking pictures'?

3 Which politician said (in 1980): 'I am not interested in a third party. I do not believe that it has any future'?

4 Which film-maker said in 1926: 'Speaking movies are impossible. When a century has passed, all thought of our so-called "talking pictures" will have been abandoned'?

5 Which rock guitarist said, 'Once you're dead, you're made for life' – and proved how right he was in 1970?

6 Which politician said in 1973: 'I would not wish to be Prime Minister, dear'?

7 Which politician said in 1973: 'The thought of being President frightens me, and I do not think I want the job'?

8 Which politician assured voters, 'Your boys are not going to be sent into any foreign wars', a year before they were?

9 Twenty-four hours before being killed, who said: 'Even if I die in the service of this nation, I would be proud of it'?

10 Sir Herbert Beerbohm Tree said of a new invention: 'It adds a new terror to life and makes death a long-felt want.' What was it?

PUT DOWNS

1 A well-known lesbian author was described as 'looking like Lady Chatterley above the waist and the game-keeper below.' Who was she?

2 Who told Harold Laski, Chairman of the Labour Party in 1945, that 'a period of silence on your part would be welcome'?

3 Who was 'a beast, but a just beast'?

4 When the Germans told him to surrender, what did 'Old Crock' McAuliffe reply?

5 Who was described by Churchill as 'Posing as a fakir of a type well-known in the East, striding half-naked up the steps of the Vice-Regal Palace'?

6 Who, according to Disraeli, was 'Never a gentleman'?

7 To which actor did Noel Coward say, 'If you weren't the best light comedian in the country, all you'd be fit for would be the selling of cars in Great Portland Street'?

8 What did Dorothy Parker say when she was told that Calvin Coolidge had died?

9 To which budding British female politician did Nancy Astor say: 'You'll never get on in politics, my dear, with *that* hair.'

10 'Being attacked by Sir Geoffrey Howe is like being savaged by a —— ——.' (Denis Healey)

QUOTERS

1 Who quoted Paul Revere in front of a Hollywood audience in 1982?

2 Who quoted from the song 'Maggie May' without knowing who Maggie May was or what she did?

3 Which politician alluded to the title of the film *Somebody Up There Likes Me* in 1983 – and why?

4 Sir Peter Hall wrote in his diary for 30 December 1973: 'The holidays feel over. Back into the world of telegrams and anger.' To what novel was he alluding?

5 Australian Prime Minister Malcolm Fraser was famous for saying the phrase 'Life is not meant to be easy' – where did he say he got it from?

6 Lord Reith used to say that the best form of government was 'despotism tempered by assassination'. Where did he get that from?

7 Adlai Stevenson, conceding the 1952 Presidential election, was quoting from whom when he said he felt like the little boy who had stubbed his toe in the dark, 'He was too old to cry, but it hurt too much to laugh'?

8 From where did Home Secretary William Whitelaw get the phrase 'short, sharp shock'?

9 Harold Macmillan chose a motto for Downing Street: 'Quiet calm deliberation disentangles every knot.' Where did he take it from?

10 Churchill said of the abdication of Edward VIII: 'He nothing common did or mean/Upon that memorable scene.' To which other king was he alluding?

RELIGION

. . . and religious folk . . .

1 What religious leader defended his liking for alcohol by saying: 'I'm so holy that when I touch wine, it turns into water'?

2 What did the 1631 'Wicked Bible' tell you to do in Exodus 20?

3 Preaching at a service to mark the Queen's Silver Jubilee in 1977, who began: 'As Jesus said – and how right he was . . .'

4 At whose memorial service at Liverpool Cathedral in 1949 was the following text used: 'God hath made me to laugh so that all who hear will laugh with me'?

5 Who said, 'Too much religion makes me go pop!'?

6 Where would you find: 'God tempers the wind to the shorn lamb'?

7 Who said: 'I look upon all the world as my parish'?

8 Who said: 'I want you to get up out of your seats, right now'?

9 'Next year in Jerusalem' – who said this?

10 If you don't know the answers to any of the above, put 'See Psalm 139, verse 6'. Why?

ROYALTY

1 When did the Queen say, 'Come on, Margaret!'?

2 Which member of the Royal Family said: 'There is no romance between us' – and announced an engagement a few days later?

3 Which member of the Royal Family said – when younger – 'I should like to be a horse'?

4 Why did Queen Elizabeth the Queen Mother observe: 'The salmon are striking back'?

5 Who said: 'I'm not particularly maternal – it's an occupational hazard of being a wife'?

6 Why did Elizabeth Andrews say: 'Bloody hell, Ma'am, what's he doing here?'

7 Who was 'Pretty amazing!'?

8 In which of her Christmas broadcasts did the Queen first say: 'My husband and I'?

9 Who said of the Queen's style of speaking that it was: 'Frankly, a pain in the neck'?

10 What, according to Disraeli, should you 'lay on with a trowel' when dealing with Royalty?

30

SEX

1 Who, when asked whether the first person he had ever slept with was a man or a woman, replied, 'I was far too polite to ask'?

2 Who said, 'Love is two minutes fifty-two seconds of squishing noises' – though he later revised it to five?

3 Who wrote of 'the love that dare not speak its name'?

4 Whose idea of extreme rudeness was 'Pee po bum belly drawers'?

5 In which novel was the heroine asked, after intercourse, 'Did thee feel the earth move?'

6 In which novel does the heroine ask, 'Where do the noses go? I always wondered where the noses would go'?

7 'His Grace returned from the wars today and pleasured me twice in his top-boots' – who was it doing it to whom?

8 Which fictional character proposed marriage in New College Lane, Oxford, with the words, 'Placetne, magistra?'

9 A man told Enid Bagnold that 'Sex is the gateway to life,' so she 'went through the gateway in an upper room at the Café Royal'. Who was he?

10 Who claimed, 'I have made love to ten thousand women'?

31

SHAKESPEARE

1 'Brevity is the soul of wit' occurs in which play?

2 'Now my charms are all o'erthrown' – says who?

3 Complete this line from Sonnet 2: 'When ——— summers shall besiege thy brow.'

4 In which Shakespeare play will you *not* find the line 'Off with his head – so much for Buckingham!'?

5 Which play ends, 'Come the three corners of the world in arms/And we shall shock them. Nought shall make us rue/If England to itself do rest but true'?

6 Which play ends, 'We that are young,/Shall never see so much, nor live so long'?

7 'Exit, pursued by a bear' is a stage direction from which play?

8 'Holding Volumnia by the hand, silent' is a stage direction from which play?

9 In which play are 'salad days' referred to?

10 Which character's last words are 'Look there, look there'?

32

SHOUTS AND CRIES

1 What were they doing when Scottish Highlanders said, 'God Bless the Duke of Argyll'?

2 Who would say, 'Worra-worra-worra'?

3 When did they shout, 'Tora, tora, tora'?

4 Where would they shout, 'Fourteen hundred'?

5 Who exclaimed, 'Poop-poop'?

6 Where do they say, 'I spy strangers'?

7 Where did they say, 'Yowsir, yowsir, yowsir'?

8 Where would you encounter the instruction, 'Do not pass go'?

9 'Pieces of eight, pieces of eight', cried —— —— (name, please).

10 What does 'Banzai!' mean?

SITUATIONS

1 What was Lord Nelson holding in his right hand when he said, 'I see no ships'?

2 'It was the best of times, it was the worst of times' – what was?

3 'From today painting is dead' – why did Paul Delaroche say that?

4 What was John Hancock doing when he said, 'There, I guess King George will be able to read that'?

5 Why did Rogers Morton say, 'I'm not going to rearrange the furniture on the deck of the Titanic'?

6 'Sergeant, arrest several of these vicars' – why?

7 Why did Lillian Hellman have to say, 'I am most willing to answer all questions about myself . . . but . . . I cannot and will not cut my conscience to fit this year's fashions'?

8 When – and why – did a radio commentator exclaim, 'Oh, the humanity!'?

9 When did Dean Rusk assert, 'We're eyeball to eyeball and I think the other fellow just blinked'?

10 Why was the little boy asked, 'And when did you last see your father?'

SLOGANS

1 What is the American equivalent of 'Queen Elizabeth slept here'?

2 'Nothing over sixpence' – in which store?

3 'Worth a guinea a box' – what were?

4 'It's so bracing!' – what is?

5 The US Second Marine Raider Division had as its slogan in World War Two the phrase 'Gung ho'. What does it mean in Chinese?

6 In 1978, Howard Jarvis campaigned for California's Proposition 13 – the one that pegged taxes – using the slogan, 'I'm as mad as hell!' Where did he take it from?

7 'Not a minute on the day, not a penny off the pay' – who campaigned with this slogan?

8 'Say it with flowers' – who suggested you should?

9 'Guns before butter' – why could you call this the G-plan diet?

10 Who was the original 'Man You Love to Hate'?

35

SONGS

1 'Have a banana!' was popularly inserted after the first line of a certain song, although the composer had not put it there. What was the song?

2 'I've just had a banana with Lady Diana' – who had?

3 'The faint aroma of performing seals' is a line that occurs in which Rodgers and Hart song?

4 'I'm not a bat . . . or a moose on the loose' – what am I?

5 'I Don't Like Mondays' sang the Boom Town Rats in 1979. Why would Brenda Spencer, a San Diego schoolgirl, agree?

6 What is the third line of 'God Save the Queen'?

7 In what song would you find the words: 'My eyes are dim, I cannot see, I have not brought my specs with me?'

8 Ulysses S. Grant said, 'I only know two tunes. One of them is "—— ——" and the other isn't.' What was the tune he did name?

9 What is the title of the English version of the French song 'Comme d'habitude'?

10 'The smile of Garbo and the scent of roses' and 'the sigh of midnight trains in empty stations' are two poetic examples – of what?

SPORT

Which sport is being referred to in each case?

1 '——— is a good walk spoiled' (Mark Twain).

2 'The first ninety minutes are the most important.'

3 'Winning isn't everything, it's the only thing' (Vince Lombardi).

4 'If you can meet with Triumph and Disaster/And treat those two impostors just the same' (Kipling) – is written over the entrance arch of a certain sporting arena.

5 'Float like a butterfly, sting like a bee.'

6 'We wuz robbed' (Joe Jacobs).

7 'Nice guys finish last' (Leo Durocher).

8 'Some people think ——— is a matter of life and death . . . I can assure them it is much more serious than that.'

9 'I have always looked upon ——— as organised loafing' (William Temple).

10 'The essential thing is not to have conquered but to have fought well' (Baron Pierre de Coubertin).

TELEGRAMS AND MESSAGES

1 Who sent a card bearing the message (and spelling mistake) – 'To Oscar Wilde, posing as a somdomite'?

2 Who sent Tom Driberg – a notorious homosexual – this telegram on the occasion of his marriage – 'I hope lightning does not strike the church'?

3 What telegram containing the information 'Moustache taken off, grown a beard' led to what apprehension?

4 What were the circumstances that led to this alliterative message – 'Sighted sub, sank same'?

5 What was the occasion of the Admiralty signal 'Winston is back'?

6 Who cabled one of his war artists (who had complained of a lack of things to draw): 'Please remain. You furnish the pictures and I'll furnish the war'?

7 Which film was the line used in?

8 Who sent a telegram from Florence: 'Have moved Hotel Excelsior. Coughing myself into a Firenze'?

9 Who cabled from Venice: 'Streets full of water. Please advise'?

10 Why would you be offended if someone sent you a critical telegram with the words 'Hebrews 13:8' on it?

38

TITLES

1 Tennessee Williams took his play-title *Cat On a Hot Tin Roof* from what longer expression?

2 Sir Edward Elgar called his marches *Pomp and Circumstance* after a Shakespeare quotation. Which one?

3 Why did Irving Berlin call his musical *Call Me Madam*?

4 The title of Agatha Christie's play *The Mousetrap* is taken from Shakespeare's ———?

5 The title of Dennis Potter's TV play *Blue Remembered Hills* came from?

6 Frank Marcus's *Mrs Mouse Are You Within?* came from?

7 Willis Hall's *The Long and the Short and the Tall* came from?

8 Give the names of two West End shows that had titles taken from Flanagan and Allen songs.

9 Why is TV's *Only Fools and Horses* so called?

10 Is the TV title *Last of the Summer Wine* a quotation?

WARS

In which war:

1 Was 'Cromwell' to be used as an alarm word if invasion of Britain was imminent?

2 Did 'the thin red line' appear?

3 Did an officer say, 'To save the town it was necessary to destroy it'?

4 Did an officer say, 'Lafayette, we are here'?

5 Did Old Bill say, 'If you know a better 'ole, go to it'?

6 Did a reporter say, 'I counted them all out and I counted them all back'?

7 Were people told to 'Set Europe ablaze'?

8 Did people first cry 'Geronimo!'?

In which military engagement:

9 Did Lord Uxbridge say, 'By god, sir, I've lost my leg'?

10 Did paddle steamers, 'Make an excursion to hell and came back victorious'?

WHO SAID THAT?

1 Which famous divorcee said, 'I married for better, for worse, but not for lunch'?

2 Which famous critic said of Noel Coward, 'Forty years ago he was Slightly in Peter Pan, and you might say that he has been wholly in Peter Pan ever since'?

3 Which famous poet said of the actress Cathleen Nesbitt that she was, 'Incredibly, inordinately, devastatingly, immortally, calamitously, hearteningly, adorably beautiful'?

4 Which famous industrialist said, 'People can have it in any colour as long as it's black'?

5 Which two famous wits *both* said, 'England and America are two countries separated by the same language'?

6 Which avuncular figure said, 'Gaiety is the most outstanding feature of the Soviet Union'?

7 Who fell for H. G. Wells 'because his skin smelt of walnuts'?

8 'We came in peace for all mankind' – who did?

9 Which famous broadcaster quoted the shortest (two-word) sentence in the New Testament on TV?

10 Which First Sea Lord used to end his letters with phrases like, 'Yours till hell freezes' and 'Yours to a cinder' and 'Yours till charcoal sprouts'?

ANSWERS

AUTHOR! AUTHOR!

1 Edward Gibbon, author of *The Decline and Fall of the Roman Empire.*

2 Noel Coward, at the first night of *Cavalcade* in 1931.

3 John Milton in his *Areopagitica.*

4 Anthony Trollope in his *Autobiography*, published in 1883, the year after his death. He shocked some readers by showing a more mercenary approach to authorship than they might have expected.

5 Sir Philip Sydney.

6 Samuel Johnson.

7 Benjamin Disraeli.

8 Christopher Isherwood in 'A Berlin Diary' from *Goodbye to Berlin.*

9 'Holden Caulfield' in J. D. Salinger's *The Catcher in the Rye.*

10 'Charlie Bubbles' in the film *Charlie Bubbles.*

BOOK TITLES

1 'Thalatta, thalatta' – Xenophon.

2 From the title song of Alan Jay Lerner's *Camelot*.

3 The English title of a Tchaikowsky song (taken from Goethe) – also known as 'None But the Weary Heart'.

4 Taken from a review of *Of Human Bondage* in the *Times Literary Supplement* – 'So busy yearning for the moon that he never saw the sixpence at his feet.'

5 From, 'That is the end of the world news', said by newsreaders on the BBC World Service.

6 'My heart is a lonely hunter that hunts on a lonely hill' – William Sharp, *The Lonely Hunter*.

7 Based on 'Now, *gods* stand up for bastards' – the Bastard Edmund in Shakespeare's *King Lear*.

8 From the Nurse in Shakespeare's *Romeo and Juliet*.

9 'Ancestral voices prophesying war' – *Kubla Khan* by Samuel Taylor Coleridge.

10 From the opening words of the Balfour Declaration which was addressed to the 2nd Lord Rothschild, the subject of the biography.

3

CATCHPHRASES

1 Michael Caine.

2 John McEnroe.

3 Kenny Everett.

4 From the TV series *Rawhide* – Frankie Laine sang the song.

5 The Daleks in *Dr Who*.

6 Hurree Jamset Ram Singh in Frank Richards's Billy Bunter stories.

7 Yosser Hughes in Alan Bleasdale's *The Boys from the Blackstuff*.

8 Political prisoner No. 6 in *The Prisoner*.

9 PC 49, in the radio series.

10 Beloved of Humphrey Bogart impersonators, but never actually said by him in *Casablanca*.

CELEBRITIES

1 W. H. Auden.

2 Charles Laughton.

3 J. M. Barrie (he posed the question to H. G. Wells).

4 Randolph Churchill.

5 David Niven.

6 J. B. Priestley.

7 Sir Huw Wheldon.

8 Rod Stewart.

9 Cyril Smith.

10 Mandy Rice-Davies.

CHURCHILLIANA

1 Charles de Gaulle.

2 Picasso.

3 Not quite. 'Never in the *field* of human conflict *was* so much owed by so many to so few.'

4 Sir Anthony Eden's.

5 When he was an old man, someone had pointed out to him that his fly-buttons were undone.

6 Clement Attlee.

7 Ramsay MacDonald.

8 'Unaccustomed as I am to public speaking' – in 1897.

9 His portrait painted by Graham Sutherland.

10 President Kennedy quoting Ed Murrow.

6

COMPLETE THE QUOTE

1 '. . . nasty, brutish, and short.'

2 '. . . baloney.'

3 '. . . good for the country' (America). (In fact, he didn't actually say it, though this is how he is usually reported.)

4 '. . . don't bump into the furniture.'

5 '. . . some animals are more equal than others.'

6 '. . . the dog it was that died.'

7 '. . . level of incompetence.'

8 '. . . Thou.'

9 '. . . France has not lost the war.'

10 '. . . that will have me as a member.'

CRITICAL OPINIONS

1 *Peter Pan* in 1904.

2 Beethoven's 7th Symphony.

3 Elgar's Symphony No 1 in A Flat.

4 William Golding, winner of the 1983 Nobel Prize for Literature – of which Lundkvist was a dissenting judge.

5 *The Wind in the Willows* by Kenneth Grahame.

6 Bruce Forsyth.

7 Wagner.

8 James Joyce.

9 *Travels*.

10 *Hamlet*.

CROSSWORDS

1 Waterless (H to O).

2 Marylebone. (The M in MCC.)

3 Pram.

4 Spaghetti.

5 German measles.

6 King's Cross.

7 Honorificabilitudinitatibus. (It occurs in Act V. The anagram 'Hi ludi, F Baconis nati, tuiti orbi' is supposed by some to prove that Bacon wrote Shakespeare – 'These plays, born of F Bacon, are preserved for the world'.)

8 Tidings (TID in GS).

9 Domain (Do Ma in).

10 The Riddle of the Sphinx.

EPITAPHS

1 Dylan Thomas.

2 John Keats.

3 John Lennon, in December 1980.

4 Earl Mountbatten of Burma.

5 George Formby Snr, music-hall star.

6 Rev Dr Martin Luther King Jnr, 1968.

7 Nurse Edith Cavell.

8 David Garrick.

9 Jonathan Swift.

10 'Even in Arcadia am I' (I = Death – it doesn't mean 'I, being a dead person, am in Arcadia'.)

FAMOUS PHRASES

1 Tennyson, *In Memoriam* (1850).

2 Adolf Hitler, in a speech, 1934.

3 Guy Fawkes, 1605.

4 Title of a book by William B. Pitkin, 1932.

5 William Faulkner – one of his phrases, used as the title of a film (1958).

6 From a 1952 song.

7 'Things Ain't What They Used To Be' – the musical composition by Mercer Ellington and Ted Persons.

8 (Florence Nightingale) Longfellow, *Santa Filomena*, 1858.

9 (Africa) Title of a book by H. M. Stanley, the one who greeted Dr Livingstone.

10 Arthur Marshall, on a late 1930s record called 'The Games Mistress'.

11

FILM QUOTES

1 *Star Wars* – the words appear on a rolling caption.

2 *The Last Remake of Beau Geste* – said to Ann-Margret whom he has just remade.

3 *Hell's Angels* – spoken by Jean Harlow.

4 *Gone With The Wind* – by Clark Gable. The book does not have the 'Frankly, my dear'.

5 *Anna Christie* – spoken by Greta Garbo.

6 *Fire Over England* – spoken by Flora Robson as Queen Elizabeth I, who actually said 'heart and stomach of a king'.

7 *E.T.*

8 *The Private Life of Henry VIII* – just before getting into bed with one of his brides.

9 *Silent Movie* – the only spoken line in the film.

10 *Song Without End* – though it wasn't in when I last saw it.

FILM TITLES

1 Shakespeare, *Cymbeline*, II, iii: 'Hark! hark! the lark at heaven's gate sings.'

2 Marlowe, *The Jew of Malta*: 'Fornication: but that was in another country/And beside the wench is dead.'

3 Oliver Goldsmith, *The Deserted Village*.

4 *The Kingdom of God* by the English poet Francis Thompson, 1913 (who spelt it 'splendoured').

5 Mary Hayley Bell thought it up herself, although it occurs in Shakespeare as 'I'd whistle her off and let her down the wind' (a hawking metaphor from *Othello*, III, iii).

6 Second witch in Shakespeare's *Macbeth*: 'By the pricking of my thumbs, something wicked this way comes.'

7 'Angels' was RAF Second World War slang for height measured in units of one thousand feet; 'One Five' stands for fifteen thousand feet.

8 William Blake, *Milton* (better known as *Jerusalem*): 'Bring me my chariot of fire' (note the singular; the plural form occurs in 2 Kings 6:17).

9 *The Book of Common Prayer*, 'Form of Prayer to be Used at Sea': '. . . and the Fleet in which we serve'.

10 Shakespeare, *King Henry IV, Part II*, III, ii: 'We have heard the chimes at midnight, Master Shallow.'

FIRST WORDS

1 (1) Edward Bulwer-Lytton's novel *Paul Clifford*, 1830; (2) the world's greatest one-line novel, written by Snoopy; (3) a child's never-ending story.

2 J. R. Ackerley, *My Father and Myself*.

3 The explosion of the first atomic bomb, 1945. He was director of the Los Alamos laboratory which produced the bomb. He was quoting from the Bhagavad Gita.

4 '. . . old Man of Lochnagar.' From the children's story by the Prince of Wales.

5 Francis Crick, on finding the structure of DNA, the basic ingredient of the genes in the cells of all living organisms.

6 *Love Story* by Erich Segal, 1970.

7 Richard Nixon and Watergate. These words come from President Ford's inaugural address in 1974.

8 Alexander Graham Bell in 1876.

9 Samuel Morse, inventor of the telegraph and the Morse Code. Other messages had been sent before this.

10 Edmund Hillary on being the first to reach the summit of Mount Everest in 1953.

FOOD

1 Pea.

2 Cucumber.

3 Trifles.

4 A madeleine (small sponge cake) – in Marcel Proust's *A La Recherche du Temps Perdu*.

5 Breakfast.

6 Water melon.

7 Hot dog.

8 Watercress sandwich.

9 Egg ('Parts of it are excellent.').

10 Jelly beans.

JUST FANCY THAT

1 Adolf Hitler, though he thought it came from Clausewitz.

2 Enoch Powell, based on Genesis 22:8.

3 Malcolm Muggeridge, from William Blake, *The Everlasting Gospel*.

4 'If the doors of perception were cleansed, every thing would appear to man as it is, infinite' – William Blake, *The Marriage of Heaven and Hell*.

5 (1) It comes from Shakespeare's *Henry V* – ''Tis not the balm, the sceptre and the ball,/The sword, the mace, the crown imperial' – as Walton once said; (2) It comes from William Dunbar – 'In beauty bearing the crown imperial' – which is what is written on the score . . .

6 False. It was so described by an American, Frederick R. Barnard, in 1927, but he made it up himself.

7 True. He said it at a railway station in South Australia.

8 King George V.

9 *Kubla Khan* (Coleridge) – she in the film *Xanadu*, they in their LP 'Welcome To The Pleasure Dome'.

10 'That's one small step for *a* man, one giant leap for mankind' (the 'a' got left out or was inaudible).

LAST WORDS

1 John Le Mesurier, the actor, in 1983.

2 Frank Sinatra at his 'farewell concert' in 1971.

3 The Mickey Mouse cartoon that was showing on BBC Television when war was declared in 1939. It was cut off before it finished.

4 'Farce'.

5 Stanley Holloway.

6 Isadora Duncan (who died when the scarf got caught in the wheels of the car she was travelling in).

7 Nancy, Lady Astor.

8 Adolf Zukor and Eubie Blake.

9 Fu Manchu, in the film *The Face of Fu Manchu*.

10 Kenneth Clark said them at the end of his TV series *Civilisation* in 1969. Lord Clark died in 1983.

17

MISQUOTES

1 'Home is the sailor, home from sea' (it said 'from *the* sea').

2 'They shall grow not old, as we that are left grow old' (it said 'not grow old').

3 It's '*rule* the waves' and '*will* be slaves'.

4 No, the Italian should translate as: 'All hope abandon, ye who enter here'.

5 No, 'For auld lang syne' is quite sufficient.

6 He went on to say, 'They wore clogs, because they lasted longer.'

7 The words are from Longfellow's *The Day is Done*.

8 'We are the masters at the moment, and not only at the moment, but for a very long time to come.'

9 'Water, water everywhere/Nor any drop to drink' – Coleridge, *The Ancient Mariner*.

10 'Tomorrow to fresh woods and pastures new' – Milton, *Lycidas*.

18

MOTTOES

1 On the rim of a £1 coin (meaning 'an ornament and a safeguard').

2 Lloyd's of London. Loose translation of 'fidentia'.

3 The Hell Fire Club; Rabelais; Aleister Crowley.

4 Richard Ingrams, editor of *Private Eye*.

5 Round Table Clubs.

6 The Royal Canadian Mounted Police (the Mounties).

7 The SAS (Special Air Service) Regiment.

8 Tesco stores – founded by Sir John *Cohen*.

9 Butlin's at Skegness, the first opened. The quote is from Shakespeare's *A Midsummer Night's Dream*.

10 The FBI.

NEWS HEADLINES

1 Arthur Miller's marriage to Marilyn Monroe.

2 Well, you see, there was this scientist called Dr Emil Fuchs and he went to Antarctica . . .

3 President Truman actually beat his challenger Thomas E. Dewey in 1948 though the paper had confidently thought otherwise.

4 Mrs Wallis Simpson (King Edward VIII's moll) was divorced (after Reno, Nevada) in Ipswich (where Cardinal Wolsey was born) in 1936.

5 The sinking of the Argentine cruiser *General Belgrano* during the Falklands War, 1982.

6 Rural audiences do not care for films with rural themes.

7 Gerry Queen was a Crystal Palace football club centre forward.

8 The Scotland football team was defeated in the World Cup.

9 The Stock Market crash of 1929.

10 Claud Cockburn claimed this was his entry in a competition for writing the dullest headline possible – though there are doubts as to whether it was ever actually printed.

PLACES

1 Hull; Halifax.

2 Sidcup.

3 Greece; Rome.

4 Switzerland.

5 Canada.

6 Giant's Causeway, Co. Antrim, Northern Ireland.

7 Greenland; Australia.

8 London.

9 Manchester.

10 Melbourne.

POETRY

1 *The Ancient Mariner* by Samuel Taylor Coleridge.

2 Sir Francis Rose (alluded to in Gertrude Stein's *Sacred Emily*) was a painter.

3 Stevie Smith, in her poem of that name.

4 Leo Marks wrote the poem that begins with these words as the basis of a code for the Special Operations Executive in the Second World War.

5 Alfred Austin (attributed). About the 1871 illness of the future Edward VII.

6 Sir John Betjeman.

7 Robert Browning (in *The Lost Leader*) about William Wordsworth whom he considered to have lost his revolutionary zeal.

8 10,000.

9 7; 'such quantities of sand' (in Lewis Carroll's *The Walrus and the Carpenter*).

10 9.

22

POLITICS

1 David Lloyd George.

2 On the steps of Parliament House in Canberra, having just been dismissed as Prime Minister by the Governor-General, in 1975.

3 The US Vice-Presidency which he held for two terms under F. D. Roosevelt.

4 Sir Douglas – later Earl – Haig, in 1918.

5 Quintin Hogg, formerly Viscount Hailsham, now Lord Hailsham.

6 Nikita S. Khruschev, in 1956.

7 Jeremy Thorpe, in a letter to Norman Scott, 1961, revealed 1976.

8 William Ewart Gladstone.

9 Alexander Dubcek, Czech leader during the 'Prague Spring', 1968.

10 Norman Tebbit, Tory politician. So he said in 1981.

23

PRESIDENTS

1 Jimmy Carter, on a visit to the north-east of England.

2 Harry S Truman – usually, 'If you can't stand the heat get out of the kitchen.'

3 Jimmy Carter.

4 John F. Kennedy.

5 Gerald R. Ford.

6 Richard M. Nixon.

7 Lyndon B. Johnson (in 1968).

8 Ronald Reagan (in 1964).

9 Lyndon B. Johnson (when Senate Majority Leader).

10 Franklin D. Roosevelt (in 1933).

PRIME MINISTERS

1 Georges Clemenceau.

2 David Lloyd George.

3 Ramsay MacDonald.

4 Stanley Baldwin.

5 Andrew Bonar Law.

6 Clement Attlee.

7 Harold Wilson.

8 Harold Macmillan.

9 Sir Alec Douglas-Home (then Lord Dunglass).

10 Arthur Balfour.

PROPHETIC REMARKS

1 Neville Chamberlain.

2 Thomas Edison.

3 Shirley Williams – who helped found the SDP in 1981.

4 D. W. Griffith.

5 Jimi Hendrix, who died from a drug overdose in 1970.

6 Margaret Thatcher.

7 Ronald Reagan.

8 President Roosevelt in 1940.

9 Indira Gandhi, assassinated in 1984.

10 The gramophone.

PUT DOWNS

1 Vita Sackville-West.

2 Clement Attlee, the then Prime Minister.

3 Dr Frederic Temple, Headmaster of Rugby School (1857–69), according to Anon.

4 'Nuts.'

5 Mahatma Gandhi.

6 William Gladstone.

7 Rex Harrison.

8 'How can they tell?'

9 Shirley Williams.

10 'Dead sheep.'

QUOTERS

1 Accepting an Oscar for his *Chariots of Fire* screenplay, Colin Welland declared, 'The British are coming.'

2 Margaret Thatcher in 1983. Maggie May was a Liverpool tart who used to steal her punters' trousers.

3 Neil Kinnock said, 'Someone up there likes me,' when his car overturned and he survived, shortly before being elected Leader of the British Labour Party.

4 E. M. Forster, *Howard's End*, chapter 19.

5 Bernard Shaw, *Back to Methuselah*.

6 A Russian noble said it to Count Munster about the assassination of Emperor Paul I in 1800.

7 Abraham Lincoln.

8 W. S. Gilbert, *The Gondoliers*.

9 W. S. Gilbert, *The Mikado*.

10 Charles I (lines from Andrew Marvell's *Upon Cromwell's Return from Ireland*).

RELIGION

1 The Aga Khan III, grandfather of the present one.

2 'Thou shalt commit adultery.'

3 Donald Coggan, Archbishop of Canterbury.

4 Tommy Handley, comedian.

5 Rosalind, wife of Robert Runcie, Archbishop of Canterbury.

6 Laurence Sterne's *Sentimental Journey* and earlier proverbial use – but not in the Bible.

7 John Wesley, founder of Methodism.

8 Dr Billy Graham, evangelist.

9 It is the traditional cry of Jews on Passover eve, seeking an end to their exile. After the 1967 reunification of Jerusalem it became, in a sense, a reality.

10 It says: 'Such knowledge is too wonderful for me . . . I cannot attain unto it.'

ROYALTY

1 At the end of a broadcast in *Children's Hour*, 1940 (to Princess Margaret).

2 Princess Anne, in 1973.

3 The Queen.

4 When a fishbone lodged in her throat, 1982.

5 Princess Anne, when expecting her second child, 1981.

6 Reacting to the intruder in the Queen's bedroom, 1982 – she being the chambermaid.

7 Prince Charles – according to Lady Diana Spencer, when she first met him.

8 The second one in 1953.

9 Lord Altrincham (1958).

10 Flattery.

30

SEX

1 Gore Vidal.

2 Johnny Rotten, formerly of The Sex Pistols.

3 Lord Alfred Douglas.

4 Michael Flanders in 'A Very Rude Song'.

5 Ernest Hemingway, *For Whom the Bell Tolls*.

6 Ditto.

7 The 1st Duke of Marlborough did to his wife, Sarah.

8 Lord Peter Wimsey. Harriet Vane accepted him with 'Placet'.

9 Frank Harris.

10 Georges Simenon.

SHAKESPEARE

1 *Hamlet*.

2 Prospero in *The Tempest*.

3 Forty.

4 *Richard III* – it was added in the eighteenth century by Colly Cibber.

5 *King John*, spoken by the Bastard.

6 *King Lear*, spoken by Albany.

7 *The Winter's Tale*.

8 *Coriolanus*.

9 *Antony and Cleopatra*.

10 King Lear.

SHOUTS AND CRIES

1 Scratching themselves – after one such Duke had erected rubbing posts for cattle in a treeless area.

2 Tigger in A. A. Milne's Pooh stories.

3 During the attack on Pearl Harbour, 1941. It was the Japanese code expression for a successful attack. Tora = tiger.

4 The London Stock Exchange when a stranger stepped on to the trading floor. Dating from the time when there were 1,399 members.

5 Mr Toad, describing the joys of motoring, in *The Wind in the Willows* by Kenneth Grahame.

6 In the House of Commons, when an MP wishes to draw attention to strangers he wants to have excluded.

7 In US dance-halls between the wars (as in *They Shoot Horses, Don't They?*). It was an expression used by the orchestra leader and entertainer, Ben Bernie. It meant 'yes, sir'.

8 On a chance card in Monopoly, the board game.

9 Captain Flint, Long John Silver's parrot in *Treasure Island* by Robert Louis Stevenson.

10 'May you live ten thousand years' (referring to the Emperor of Japan).

SITUATIONS

1 Nothing. He did not have one. The telescope which he put to his blind (right) eye would have had to be in his left hand.

2 The French Revolution – the opening words of *A Tale of Two Cities* by Charles Dickens.

3 On hearing of Daguerre's invention – the daguerreotype – an early photographic process, 1838.

4 Signing the American Declaration of Independence in 1776 with the biggest signature of all.

5 As an aide of President Ford, he was not going to make any last-ditch attempts to salvage the President's re-election campaign in 1976.

6 (Actually, it should be, 'Sergeant, arrest most of these people.') Impossible to explain why briefly, but it occurs in Philip King's farce *See How They Run* when most of the cast are – or are dressed as – vicars.

7 She was refusing to testify against friends about their alleged communist leanings before the House Committee on Un-American Activities in 1952.

8 When the German airship *Hindenburg* burst into flame while he was describing the scene in 1937 and passengers fell to the ground.

9 During the 1962 Cuban missile crisis, when the Soviet Union gave way. He was US Secretary of State.

10 Of Cavalier family, he was being questioned by Roundheads, in the painting by W. F. Yeames, 1878.

SLOGANS

1 'George Washington slept here'.

2 Woolworth's, before the Second World War.

3 Beecham's Pills.

4 Skegness, the seaside resort, according to John Hassall's jolly bouncing fisherman poster.

5 'Work together'.

6 The film *Network* where the pundit–evangelist says, 'I'm as mad as hell, and I'm not going to take this anymore!'

7 The National Union of Mineworkers, prior to the 1926 General Strike.

8 The Society of American Florists, from 1918, followed by many others.

9 Both Goebbels and Goering, Nazi leaders, made use of the slogan in 1936.

10 Eric von Stroheim, billed as such for the 1918 film *The Heart of Humanity*.

SONGS

1 'Let's All Go Down the Strand' (1904).

2 'Burlington Bertie from Bow' (1915).

3 'I Wish I Were In Love Again'.

4 'I am a mole and I live in a hole' – from 'The Mole in the Hole', a record by The Southlanders in 1956.

5 She gave this reason for murdering her school principal and a custodian, and wounding nine others, thus inspiring the song-writer.

6 'God save the queen' (not 'our').

7 'In the Quartermaster's Store'.

8 'Yankee Doodle'.

9 'My Way'.

10 'These foolish things . . . that remind me of you' (Eric Maschwitz).

SPORT

1 Golf.

2 Football. (Bobby Robson, England manager.)

3 US pro-football.

4 Tennis. (The centre court at Wimbledon.)

5 Boxing. (Muhammad Ali's 'credo'.)

6 Boxing. (Jacobs was manager of Max Schmeling and in 1932 shouted this remark when he felt the boxer had been cheated of a title.)

7 Baseball. (He was manager of the Brooklyn Dodgers.)

8 Football. (Bill Shankly, manager, 1973.)

9 Cricket.

10 Any of the Olympic sports.

37

TELEGRAMS & MESSAGES

1 The Marquis of Queensberry, in 1895 – the action that led to Wilde charging Queensberry with making and publishing a criminal libel.

2 Evelyn Waugh.

3 The arrest of the murderer, Dr Crippen, on a ship trying to escape to Canada.

4 The first US naval success in the Second World War was the sinking of a Japanese submarine. Pilot Donald Mason reported it thus.

5 Churchill's return to the Admiralty in September 1939 (he'd been there in the First World War).

6 William Randolph Hearst in 1898.

7 *Citizen Kane.*

8 Noel Coward.

9 Robert Benchley.

10 The passage states: 'Jesus Christ, the same yesterday, and today, and forever.'

38

TITLES

1 'As nervous as a cat on a hot tin roof'.

2 'Pride, pomp and circumstance of glorious war' – Othello says it to Iago.

3 (It was about a woman US ambassador.) From a misquotation of something never said by Frances Perkins, the first American woman to reach Cabinet rank (1934). She had been asked how she was to be addressed in Cabinet.

4 *Hamlet*.

5 A. E. Housman, *A Shropshire Lad*.

6 From the nursery rhyme 'A Frog He Would A-Wooing Go'.

7 From the song 'Bless 'Em All' and its parody 'Sod 'Em All'.

8 'Underneath the Arches'; (Down) 'Forget-me-not Lane' (Peter Nichols).

9 From the cockney expression 'Only fools and horses work'.

10 No. Roy Clarke just called it that.

WARS

1 The Second World War.

2 The Crimean War – a phrase used by W. H. Russell to describe the British.

3 The Vietnam War.

4 The First World War, when the American Expeditionary Force arrived in France.

5 The First World War, said by Bruce Bairnsfather's character.

6 The Falklands War (BBC reporter, Brian Hanrahan).

7 The Second World War (Churchill to members of the SOE).

8 The Second World War (jumping by parachute).

9 The Battle of Waterloo (he later became 1st Marquess of Anglesey).

10 During the retreat from Dunkirk (in the words of J. B. Priestley).

WHO SAID THAT?

1 The Duchess of Windsor (explaining why, when the Duke stayed at home for lunch, she often went out).

2 Kenneth Tynan.

3 Rupert Brooke. (She had complained he got 'drunk on words'.)

4 Henry Ford on the Model T Ford motor car.

5 Bernard Shaw and Oscar Wilde – the latter in the form, 'We have really everything in common with America nowadays, except, of course, language.'

6 'Uncle Joe' Stalin.

7 Rebecca West.

8 The first men on the moon left a plaque bearing these words, 1969.

9 Richard Dimbleby said, 'Jesus wept' (John 11:35), on live TV, May 1965.

10 Admiral Lord Fisher.

Also available in Unwin Paperbacks